This book is given to

_____

from

_____

Whom God Has Joined Together

Words to Stay Married By

Helen Caswell

DIMENSIONS
FOR LIVING
NASHVILLE

Whom God Has Joined Together

ISBN 0-687-01009-8

Scripture quotations, unless otherwise noted, are from the King James Version of the Bible.

Scripture quotations noted RSV are from the Revised Standard Version of the Bible, copyright © 1946, 1952, 1971 by the Division of Christian Education of the National Council of the Churches of Christ in the U.S.A. Used by permission.

97 98 99 00 01 02 03 04 05 06—10 9 8 7 6 5 4 3 2 1

Printed in Hong Kong

Whom God
Has Joined
Together

Dedication

In golden candlelight, friends old and new, from near and far, wished us well as we celebrated our fiftieth wedding anniversary. In a pause in the conversation a clear young voice asked,

"Granny, have you any words of wisdom about how to be happily married after fifty years?"

It was a serious request. Our eldest granddaughter was engaged to be married.

"I'll give it some thought," I told her, "and you shall have a whole book of words of wisdom."

So here it is—for Dondi Caswell Barlay and also, of course, for my husband, with love.

Helen Caswell
Winter Creek Farm
1994

Learning to Love

. . . when we love,
we must not forget
that we are
beginners,
bunglers of life,
apprentices
in love, and we must
learn to love,
with calm and
patience.

—*Rainer Maria Rilke*

*L*ove is patient and kind;
love is not jealous or boastful;
it is not arrogant or rude.
Love does not insist on its
own way; it is not irritable
or resentful; it does not rejoice
at wrong, but rejoices in the right.
Love bears all things,
believes all things,
hopes all things,
endures all things.
Love never ends. . . .
Faith, hope, love abide;
these three,
but the greatest of these
is love.

1 Corinthians 13:4-8a, 13 RSV

Delige et quod vis fac.
(Love and do what you will.)

St. Augustine

In Tove Jansson's "The Summer Book"
the child Sophia is hopelessly
enamored of a cat who does not
return her affection.

"It's funny about love,"
Sophia said. "The more you
love some-one, the less he
loves you back."
"That's very true,"
grandmother observed.
"And so what do you do?"
"You go on loving," Sophia said
threateningly, "you love harder and
harder."

Her grandmother sighed, and said nothing.

He who binds to himself a joy
Does the winged life destroy;
But he who kisses the joy as it flies
Lives in eternity's sunrise.

William Blake

Love doesn't just sit there, like a stone,
it has to be made, like bread,
remade all the time, made new.

Ursula K. LeGuin

People talk about love as though it were
something you could give, like an armful
of flowers.

Anne Morrow Lindbergh

The world waits for love—
the vigilance of love,
the service of love,
the sacrifice of love.

Bishop Henry C. Potter

Let me not to the marriage of true minds
Admit impediments. Love is not love
Which alters when it alteration finds,
Or bends with the remover to remove:
Oh, no! it is an ever-fixed mark,
That looks on tempests and is never shaken;
It is the star to every wandering bark,
Whose worth's unknown, although his height be taken.
Love's not Time's fool, though rosy lips and cheeks
Within his bending sickle's compass come;
Love alters not with his brief hours and weeks,
But bears it out even to the edge of doom.
If this be error and upon me prov'd,
I never writ, nor no man ever lov'd.

William Shakespeare

He that loveth not
knoweth not God;
for God is love.
1 John 4:8

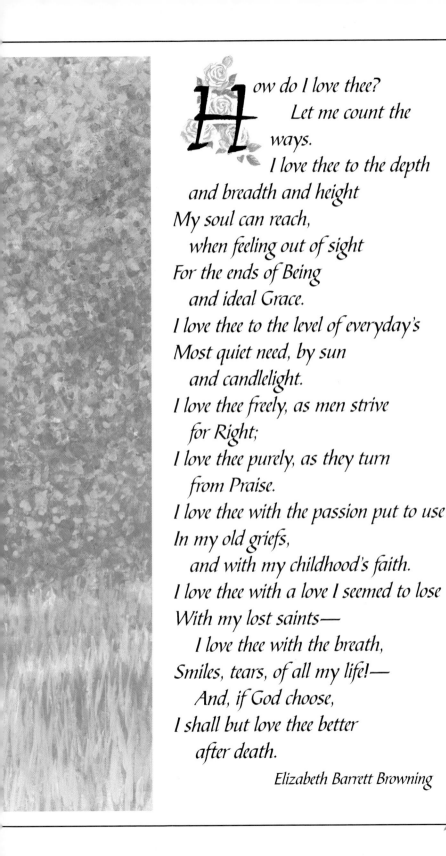

How do I love thee?
   Let me count the
   ways.
      I love thee to the depth
and breadth and height
My soul can reach,
   when feeling out of sight
For the ends of Being
   and ideal Grace.
I love thee to the level of everyday's
Most quiet need, by sun
   and candlelight.
I love thee freely, as men strive
   for Right;
I love thee purely, as they turn
   from Praise.
I love thee with the passion put to use
In my old griefs,
   and with my childhood's faith.
I love thee with a love I seemed to lose
With my lost saints—
   I love thee with the breath,
Smiles, tears, of all my life!—
   And, if God choose,
I shall but love thee better
   after death.

Elizabeth Barrett Browning

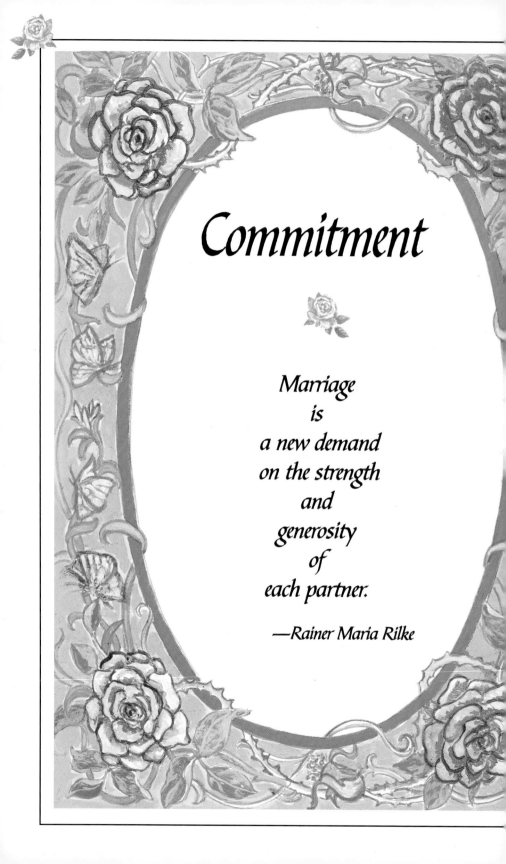

Commitment

Marriage
is
a new demand
on the strength
and
generosity
of
each partner.

—Rainer Maria Rilke

*T*hen shall the
minister say to the
woman, Wilt thou
have this man
to be thy wedded husband,
to live together
after God's ordinance in the
holy estate of matrimony?
Wilt thou love him,
    comfort him,
honour, and keep him
in sickness and health, and,
forsaking all others,
    keep thee only unto him,
    so long as ye both
    shall live?

And the woman shall answer,
I will.

From the Marriage Service

A good marriage is one
in which each partner
appoints the other to be
the guardian of his
solitude, and thus they show
each other the greatest
possible trust.

Rainer Maria Rilke

Companionship
thrives only when each individual
remembers his individuality and does
not identify himself with others.

Carl Jung

Of courtesy, it is much less
Than courage of heart or holiness,
Yet in my walks it seems to me
That the Grace of God is in courtesy.

Hilaire Belloc

Hail wedded love,
  mysterious law,
    true source
Of human offspring, sole propriety
In Paradise of all things common else.

John Milton
Paradise Lost

Some pray to marry the man they love,
  My prayer will somewhat vary;
I humbly pray to Heaven above
  That I love the man I marry.

Rose Pastor Stokes

I have met women whom I really think would
like to be married to a poem, and to be
given away by a novel.

John Keats, in a letter
to Fanny Brawne

The tragedy of marriage is that while all
women marry thinking that their man
will change, all men marry believing that
their wives will never change. Both are
invariably disappointed.

Len Deighton

It is as absurd to say that a man cannot love
one woman all the time as it is to say that a
violinist needs several violins to play the same
piece of music.

Honoré de Balzac

Blessed art Thou O Lord who
makest the Bridegroom
to rejoice with the Bride.

From a Hebrew wedding prayer

*S*ometimes a wedding is symbolic of the marriage that follows. Ours was. Inadvertently we started out as we were to go on.

We were married in a small, pretty chapel with rose-amethyst windows and a proper center aisle, decorated with sprays of heather. He had been twenty-one for almost a month and was wearing his new Navy uniform. I was nineteen and had a dress of ivory satin with a three-foot train. The lovely lady who was my music teacher played her golden harp and we had a festive reception with hundreds of friends.

And then we drove off into a pouring rain, with no hotel reservations.

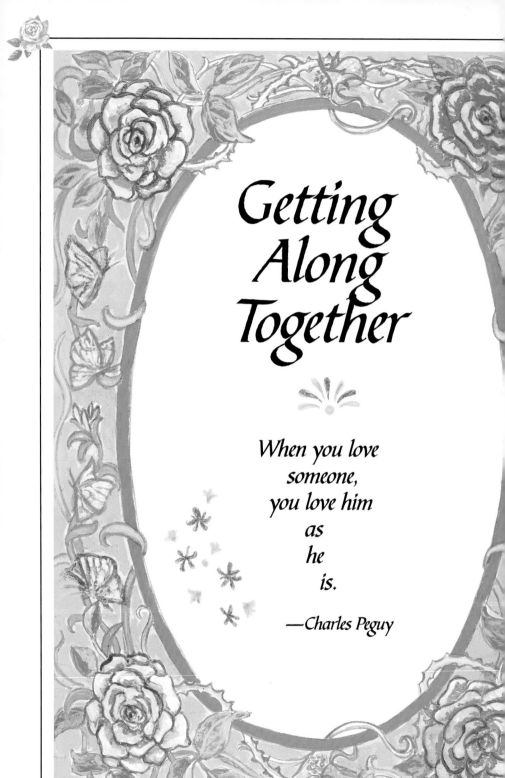

Getting Along Together

When you love
someone,
you love him
as
he
is.

—Charles Peguy

*I*s the key to love
    in passion, knowledge,
        affection?
All three—along with
    moonlight, roses, groceries,
givings and forgivings,
    gettings and forgettings,
        keepsakes and room rent,
        pearls of memory
        along with ham and eggs.
                        Carl Sandburg
                        Honey and Salt

To reduce a romantic idea
    to a working plan
        is a very difficult thing.
                    Erskine Childers

When two quarrel
    both are in the wrong.
                    Spanish proverb

Anger
    is a short madness.
                    Horace

Even our sexuality should be regarded as the transposition
into a minor key of that creative joy which in
him is unceasing and irresistible.

C. S. Lewis

Every statement our Lord made about sexuality works to protect women and to awaken men to their responsibilities. Condemning adultery, he yet forgave the adulteresses who repented and loved God, and denounced the lustful and loveless men who caused them to sin. Perhaps that, in itself, is enough to prove him more than man.

Joy Davidman Lewis

Reality is never ideal. We patch up as we go on.
We do not create things, they happen, and we
cope with them.

Julian Rathbone

The trouble with acquiring your sex education through romantic novels is you don't realize that love is miserably hard work.

Dorothy Cannell

Do not do unto others as you would they should do unto you. Their tastes may not be the same.

George Bernard Shaw

Look out how you use proud words.
When you let proud words go,
   it is not easy to call them back.
They wear long boots, hard boots;
   they walk off proud;
They can't hear you calling—
Look out how you use hard words.
                    Carl Sandburg

It is easy—terribly easy—to shake a man's faith in himself.
To take advantage of that to break a man's spirit is devil's
work.
                    George Bernard Shaw

Except in cases of necessity, which are rare, leave your friend
to learn unpleasant things from his enemies; they are ready
enough to tell him.
                    Oliver Wendell Holmes

A little silence can come as something of a relief, in the wear
and tear of marriage.
                    John Mortimer's
                    Horace Rumpole

You would be surprised to know how much unnecessary
worry a simple policy of polite disinterest can save one.
                    Margery Allingham

Let the tongue have its reins firmly in the heart.
                    Columbanus

*S*peak softly; sun going down
  Out of sight. Come near me
  now,
Dear dying fall of wings as birds
Complain against the gathering dark . . .

Exaggerate the green blood in grass;
the music of leaves scraping space;

Multiply the stillness by one sound;
By one syllable of your name . . .

And all that is little is soon giant,
All that is rare grows in common
beauty

To rest with my mouth on your mouth
As somewhere a star falls

And the earth takes it softly,
  in natural love . . .
Exactly as we take each other . . .
  and go to sleep.

Kenneth Patchen
Fall of the Evening Star

Homemaking

*Peace
be
to
this
house.*

There is a priceless ingredient which, included in even the humblest recipes, restores the weary bodies and hearts of those who eat of it, and that is love. If the cook is angry or fretful, or in great haste to get on to something else, whatever her skill, that which she prepares will be dead sea fruit, and all manner of little aches and pains will follow on the eating of it. It is well, then, to stop and remind oneself of the deep responsibility one has to preserve the health and well-being of the family, and resolutely put aside all haste and irritation while ministering to the family's needs. Unless love is there, it were better that they go hungry.

The less time one has, the more important it is to manage.

It is not the load, but thinking about
    it that makes us tired.

The Powell House Cookbook
A collection of recipes from Quaker cooks

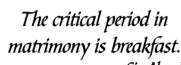

The critical period in
matrimony is breakfast.

Sir Alan Patrick Herbert

When in doubt, cook something and eat it.

Robert B. Parker

Je vis de bonne soupe et non de beau langage.
(I live on good soup and not fine language)   Molière

Whoever you are, God or anybody else, you work with the
materials at hand.   Lawrence Block

The Pennsylvania Dutch have a saying:
  Kissin' don't last; cookin' do.
And Garrison Keillor maintains that sex is good, but not as
good as fresh sweet corn.

There are few hours in life more agreeable than the hour
dedicated to . . . afternoon tea.   Henry James
                                        The Portrait of a Lady

It has long been an axiom of mine that the little things are
infinitely the most important.

Conan Doyle's Sherlock Holmes

Work is love made visible.

Kahlil Gibran
The Prophet

Most of our decisions are forced on us by
laziness.   Edmund Crispin's Gervase Fen

All the world's a stage . . . (William Shakespeare)
and the stage managers are mostly women. And the romance
of the stage is an illusion created by a lot of unromantic hard
work. If a man wants a romantic dinner by candlelight, he
makes reservations at an expensive restaurant. A woman
may not only arrange the flowers and light the candles—she
may spend hours cleaning the house and preparing Tournedos
Dauphinoise, allowing time to shower and make herself
glamorous. So—all of this stage-setting, this home-making,
is (let's face it) woman's work.
If it had been left to the men we might still be
sitting about in caves gnawing on haunches of mastodon.

A house with daffodils is a house lit up,
whether or no the sun is shining outside.
Daffodils in a green bowl—and let it snow
if it will.   A. A. Milne

The sober comfort,
all the peace
which springs
From the large aggregate
of little things;
On these small cares
of daughter, wife, or friend,
The almost sacred joys
of home depend.
                    Hannah Moore

Let all things be done
decently and in order.
                    1 Corinthians 14:40

Good order is the foundation
of all good things.
                    Edmund Burke

Order is heaven's first law.
                    Alexander Pope

Set thine house in order.
                    Isaiah 38:1

Cleanliness may not be next to
godliness, but perhaps a case
could be made for orderliness.

Parenting

*Train up a child
in the way
he should go:
and
when he is old,
he will not
depart from it.*

—Proverbs 22:6

*S*uffer the little
children to come unto
me, and forbid
them not:
for of such is the kingdom
of God.

Mark 10:14

And Jesus called a
little child unto him,
and set him in the midst of
them,
and said, "Verily, I say unto
you,
Except ye be converted,
and become as little children,
ye shall not enter into
the kingdom of heaven.
And whoso shall receive
one such little child in
my name receiveth me.

Matthew 18:2-3, 5

. . . A child left to himself bringeth his mother to shame.

Proverbs 29:15

. . . And, ye fathers, provoke not your children to wrath: but bring them up in the nurture and admonition of the Lord.

Ephesians 6:4

. . . I have lived thirty years on this planet, and I have yet to hear the first syllable of earnest advice from my seniors. *

Henry David Thoreau

*As a parent of young adults during the sixties and a bit sick of Walden Pond, my sympathies were with the seniors.
They probably gave plenty of earnest advice, but Henry David, by his own admission, didn't hear it.
As Ogden Nash said:
Children aren't happy with nothing to ignore,
And that's what parents were created for.

The truth of it is, the first rudiments of education are given very indiscreetly by most parents.

Sir Richard Steele

Children sweeten labors, but they make misfortunes more bitter.
The joys of parents are secret, and so are their griefs and fears.

Francis Bacon

And he who gives a child
a treat
Makes joy-bells ring
in heaven's street.
And he who gives a
child a home
Builds palaces
in kingdom come,
And she who gives
a baby birth
Brings Saviour Christ
again to earth.
John Masefield

Parentage is a very important profession; but no test of
fitness for it is ever imposed in the interest of the children.
George Bernard Shaw

Discipline without regimentation was Miss Bulstrud's motto.
Discipline, she said, was reassuring to the young, it gave
them a feeling of security; regimentation gave rise to irritation.
Agatha Christie
Cat Among the Pigeons

Before I got married I had six theories about bringing up
children. Now I have six children and no theories.
Earl of Rochester
John Wilmot

eople will tell you, "The years when your children are little are the happiest years of your life." This is not necessarily true. For me, the words that best express those years are to be found in A. A. Milne's *Winnie the Pooh*. Perhaps because this was one of the few books I was able to read at that time—in fact, *had* to read, over and over, I found in it depth and sustenance beyond anything Mr. Milne intended. At any rate, here is the passage in which I identified poignantly with the bear:

"Here is Edward Bear, coming downstairs now, bump, bump, bump, on the back of his head, behind Christopher Robin. It is, as far as he knows, the only way of coming downstairs, but sometimes he feels that there really is another way, if only he could stop bumping for a moment and think of it. And then he
    feels that
        perhaps
            there isn't."

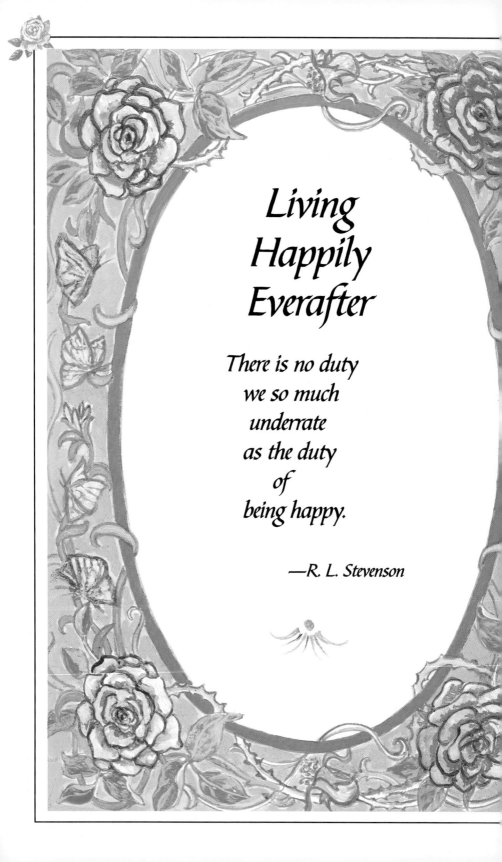

Living Happily Everafter

There is no duty
we so much
underrate
as the duty
of
being happy.

—R. L. Stevenson

J oy is the grace
we say to
God.
Jean Ingelow

Sing praises to the LORD,
O you his saints,
and give thanks to
his holy name.
For his anger is but
for a moment,
and his favor is
for a lifetime.
Weeping may tarry
for the night,
but joy comes
with the morning.
Psalm 30:4–5 RSV

. . . With an eye made
quiet by the power
of harmony,
and the deep power
of joy, we see into
the life of things.
William Wordsworth

My heart is like
a singing bird
whose nest is in a
watered shoot;
My heart is like an apple-tree
Whose boughs are bent
with thickset fruit;
My heart is like a rainbow shell
That paddles in a halcyon sea;
My heart is gladder than all these
Because my love is come to me.

Christina Rossetti
A Birthday

To the wise man every day is a festival.
Plutarch

That distrust which intrudes often on your
mind is a mode of melancholy, which, if it be
the business of a wise man to be happy, it is
foolish to indulge; and if it be a duty to
preserve our faculties entire for their proper
use, it is criminal.

Samuel Johnson, in a
letter to Boswell

Prepare for mirth, for mirth becomes a feast.
William Shakespeare, Pericles

He that is of a merry heart hath a continual feast.
Proverbs 15:15

If I have faltered more or less
In my great task of happiness,
If I have moved among my race
And shown no glorious morning face;
If beams from happy human eyes
Have moved me not; if morning skies,
Books, and my food, and summer rain
Knocked on my sullen heart in vain;—
Lord, thy most pointed pleasure take
And stab my spirit broad awake;
Or, Lord, if too obdurate I,
Choose thou, before that Spirit die,
A piercing pain, a killing sin,
And to my dead heart run them in!
               Robert Louis Stevenson
               The Celestial Surgeon

We have no more right to consume happiness
without producing it than to consume
wealth without producing it.
               George Bernard Shaw

This is the day which the LORD hath made;
we will rejoice and be glad in it.

                         Psalm 118:24

  But—
Cheerfulness
without humor
is a very trying thing.
      G. K. Chesterton

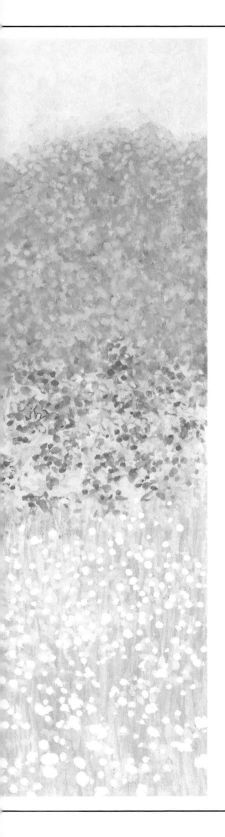

*F*or the good are
always
the merry,
Save by an evil chance,
And the merry love
the fiddle,
And the merry love to dance.
W. B. Yeats
The Fiddler of Dooney

Mix a little foolishness
with your serious plans:
it's lovely to be silly
at the right moment.
Horace

...Headlong joy
is ever on the wing.
Milton

Happiness
is no laughing matter.
Richard Whately,
Archbishop of Dublin

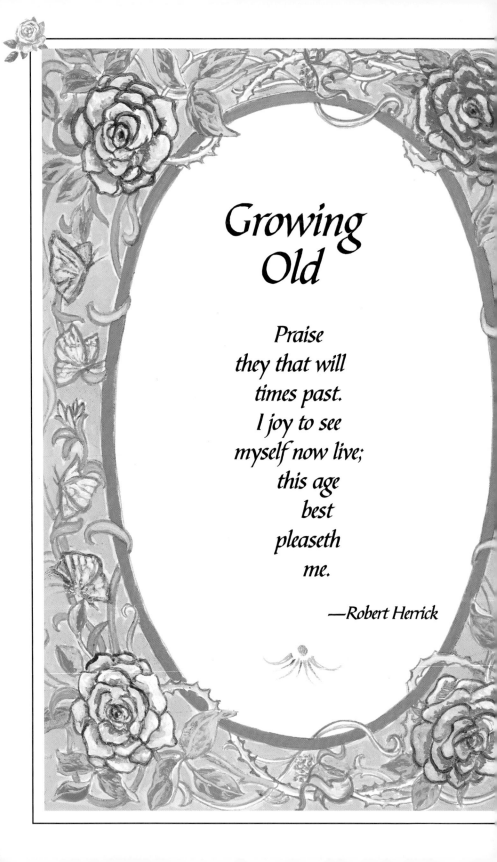

Growing Old

Praise
they that will
times past.
I joy to see
myself now live;
this age
best
pleaseth
me.

—Robert Herrick

*Grow old along
with me!
The best is yet to be,
The last of life,
for which the first was made.
Our times are in His hand
Who saith, "A whole I planned,
Youth shows but half;
trust God,
see all,
nor be afraid!"*

Robert Browning
Rabbi ben Ezra

*Is not old wine wholesomest,
old pippins toothsomest,
old wood burn brightest,
old linen wash whitest?
Old soldiers,
sweethearts,
are surest,
and old lovers are soundest.*

John Webster
Westward Ho!

Love is a circle that doth restless move In the same sweet eternity of Love. —Herrick

To be seventy
years young
is sometimes
far more
cheerful
and
hopeful
than
to be
forty
years
old.

Oliver Wendell Holmes on
the 70th birthday of
Julia Ward Howe

He hath made every thing beautiful in
his time: he hath also set the world in
their heart.

Ecclesiastes 3:11

To me, fair friend, you never can be old,
For as you were when first your eye I ey'd,
Such seems your beauty still.

William Shakespeare

There are no happy endings . . . There are only happy people.

Dorothy Gilman's Mrs. Polifax

Call him not old, whose visionary brain
Holds o'er the past its undivided reign.
For him in vain the envious seasons roll
Who bears eternal summer in the soul.

Oliver Wendell Holmes
The Old Player

The setting sun, and music at the close,
As the last taste of sweets,
    is sweetest last,
Writ in remembrance
    more than things long past.

William Shakespeare
Richard II

O my luve's like a red, red rose
    That's newly sprung in June.
O my luve's like the melody
    That's sweetly play'd in tune.
As fair art thou, my bonnie lass,
    So deep in luve am I.
And I will luve thee still, my dear,
    Till all the seas gang dry.
Till all the seas gang dry, my dear,
    And the rocks melt wi' the sun;
I will luve thee still my dear,
    While the sands o' life shall run.

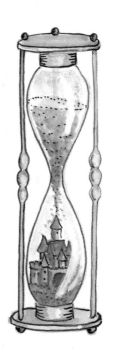

Robert Burns

Shall I compare thee
to a summer's day?
Thou art more lovely
and more temperate:
Rough winds do shake
the darling buds of May,
And summer's lease
has all too short a date:
Sometime too hot
the eye of heaven shines,
And often is his gold complexion
dimm'd;
And every fair from fair sometime
declines,
By chance or nature's
changing course untrimm'd;
But thy eternal summer shall not
fade
Nor lose possession of that fair
thou owest;
Nor shall Death brag
thou wander'st in his shade,
When in eternal lines
to time thou growest:
So long as men can breathe
or eyes can see
So long lives this
and this gives life to thee.

William Shakespeare